First published 1981 by Camden House Publishing Ltd.
publisher of *Harrowsmith* Magazine.

Text © 1981 by Carole Spray
Illustrations © 1981 By Kim La Fave

Camden House Publishing Ltd.
Queen Victoria Road
Camden East, Ontario
Canada K0K 1J0

Creative Direction: Elinor Campbell Lawrence

Design: Burns, Cooper, Hynes Limited, Toronto

Colour Separations and Printing: Herzig Somerville Limited

Binding: Bryant Press Ltd.

Originated and manufactured in Canada.

Distribution: Firefly Books Ltd.
3520 Pharmacy Avenue
Scarborough, Ontario, Canada M1W 2T8

Canadian Cataloguing in Publication Data

Spray, Carole, 1942 —
The mare's egg

ISBN 0-920656-06-4 (Hardcover)

I. La Fave, Kim, 1955 — II. Title.

PS8587 P72M37  398.2  C81-090109-9
PZ8.1.S67Ma

# The Mare's Egg

A New World Folk Tale

In memory of Ralph Amos who told me the story

retold by Carole Spray
illustrated by Kim La Fave
afterword by Margaret Atwood

Where this man came from, no one seemed to know. Certainly he was one of the many strangers coming into the country to settle. But it soon became clear that some of these newcomers, although willing enough, just weren't cut out to be pioneers. In fact, some of them didn't seem to know very much about anything at all.

Now the man I am going to tell you about was just such a person. He had got a grant of land, started himself a clearing in the forest and had built himself a small cabin. And, as was the custom, he had fashioned a big stone fireplace and chimney.

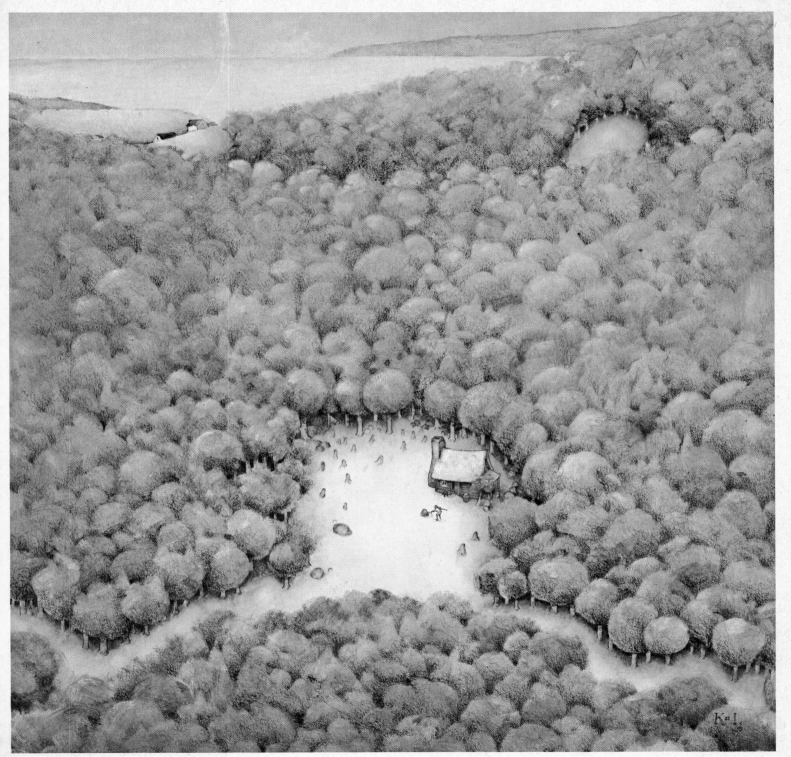

As you can imagine, this work was very heavy — pulling stumps and dragging great stones — and the man began to realize that a horse was just what he needed to help him in this new life.

e talked to his neighbours and each warned him of certain things to look for in a horse that would indicate the disposition and usefulness of the beast.

One old-timer warned him to pay very special attention to a horse's ears, for if the animal had long ears, it would be balky as an old mule.

nother neighbour cautioned him that if an animal went about baring its teeth, it would surely be a biter and apt to take a nip from his arm — or worse — if he weren't careful.

Still another advised him to watch a horse as it moved around, and, if it appeared low in the hindquarters, he should be wary of it, for such a brute was likely to be a kicker.

All agreed on one thing. He must be careful not to buy a runaway, for the minute he dropped the reins, the horse would be off across the fields, into the trees and gone forever.

To this man, it was all very confusing. In the city he had never had to worry about such matters and he began to wonder if he could ever find a horse that didn't have one bad habit or another.

One day, as the settler was walking down a country road, he spied a farmer in a field piling up a stack of pumpkins. Now as it happened, the farmer was cleaning up after his team of horses which had broken down the fence, trampled the pumpkin vines and left quite a bit of their manure around, but the newcomer knew none of this. He watched the farmer for a moment, then walked right into the garden and bid him good-day. (They were complete strangers, but in those days it was not uncommon to speak to people you didn't know.)

"Sir, just what are those, anyway?" he asked, pointing to the big ripe pumpkins.

"You don't know what these are?" asked the farmer, and if you had been watching closely, you would have seen a mischievous glint come into his eyes.

"No," admitted the settler, "I've never seen the likes of them."

"Why everyone knows what these are," said the farmer, slicing a plug of chewing tobacco and tucking a wad into his cheek.

"Mare's eggs. And as nice a lot of them as you're likely to see."

"Mare's eggs?" said the settler, with sudden interest.

"Why, yes. Just look around you here at all the flattened vines and manure. My good mare made her nest here and those are the eggs she laid."

The settler could hardly believe his good fortune. Here was a chance to get a horse *before* it could learn a single bad habit. He would buy one of these eggs, hatch out a colt and raise the young animal to behave itself from the start.

"Sell me a mare's egg," he said to the farmer, "and I'll hatch it myself."

"Well, I don't know," said the farmer. "You would have to take it home very carefully. Couldn't drop it or bang it around. It would never hatch." He spat some tobacco juice on the earth, stroked his chin whiskers thoughtfully and seemed to be having a great deal of trouble making up his mind.

"You have a fireplace, I suppose?" he said at last, looking the settler straight in the eye.

"Oh, yes!"

"Well then, it might work. You'll have to build up the fire and wrap your egg in blankets or quilts or an old coat — anything to keep it warm, you know. Then you'll have to set it in a safe spot by the fireplace."

"How long will it take to hatch?" asked the settler, and you could see that *he* was getting a gleam in *his* eye by this time.

"Oh, if you just warm it on the hearth, it will take about eight weeks. But if you want the colt sooner, you can shorten the time. Whenever you have a few spare minutes, go and sit on the egg to warm it up. The more heat it gets, the more quickly it will hatch. But remember, be *very, very* careful that when you sit down, you don't break the shell."

"ould you be kind enough to sell me one of your eggs?"

"Well, I don't see why I shouldn't . . . ."

"How much would you want for one?"

"Oh," said the farmer slowly, "do you think ten dollars is too much?"

The settler's mind was racing and he could already picture himself lolloping along the country lanes on his very own steed. He knew that he would have to pay up to one hundred and fifty dollars for a full-grown horse, and who knew if it would bite or kick or refuse to work? Ten dollars, he thought, was the best bargain he'd found since arriving in this country.

He paid the coins and the farmer asked him, "What do you have in mind — a large egg or a small one?"

The settler looked at the pumpkins, puzzled for a moment, and asked, "Is there a difference?"

"It's this way," said the farmer. "The big eggs will hatch you a big colt and it will grow to be a bigger horse, while the smaller eggs will produce a lesser colt — which may be a better horse on the road, but not near as good a brute for work. I would advise you to take a big egg, for you tell me you have so much clearing and heavy work to do."

This made good sense to the settler and he picked out the largest pumpkin in the patch, lifted it gingerly and struggled out of the field with it. He was no more than a slip of a man, probably a clerk in a bank before he decided to try the pioneering life. Still, he managed to get the huge orange load all the way home, with not so much as a single bump to harm the developing colt inside.

He took his coat and a pair of blankets from his bed to wrap around the egg and then set it where the warmth from the fire would do the most good. As his fire had died during the day, he quickly kindled a new one, then hurried out to split more wood and stack it inside so the fire would never be allowed to go out.

The man didn't even bother to fix his supper that night, but just sat right on top of the egg and mused happily about what a bargain he had made and about the fine young colt he would soon have.

D ays passed, and it was not the easiest of times for the settler. His coat and blankets were wrapped around the pumpkin and the weather was turning quite frosty. He rushed to finish his chores so that he could get back to sit on the egg, and this, too, was not easy. If you've ever tried to sit atop a mare's egg for days on end, then you'll know what I mean.

He was sure the egg would hatch at the end of six weeks — he had taken such good care of it — but nothing happened. He sat on the egg for another two weeks. Still, nothing happened.

inally, when he had sat on the egg for ten full weeks, he went to see the farmer who had sold it to him and explained his troubles.

"Well," said the farmer, scratching the back of his head, "maybe the egg is just slow in hatching. You must remember that it's been very cold weather and because of that the egg might need a little longer to hatch. These things take time."

So the settler went home to sit on the egg again and stayed there, dutiful as a mother hen, for two more weeks. Still no colt. He began to get seriously worried. Nevertheless, he was a determined man and he sat on the egg for several weeks more, watching the leaves on the trees turn from their bright fall colours to a lifeless brown. One day he noticed that nearly all the leaves had blown down, and he knew then that the egg would never hatch.

He admitted to himself that the egg he was sitting on had begun to rot and the colt must have died.

The settler made up his mind to do away with it, for he had learned that a rotten hen's egg smelled terribly and he was afraid that this giant mare's egg would get broken or burst. The smell would be simply atrocious. He might even have to abandon his little cabin until the air cleared.

Lifting the egg as carefully as he could, he went across his chopping and into the woods a short distance to a place where there was a small downhill slope. And, as is often the case, at the bottom of the grade there were thick bushes and brambles. This seemed the perfect place to rid himself of the monstrous egg.

With great effort, he raised the egg high over his head and heaved it toward the bushes at the foot of the slope. The egg hurtled through the air. Then, there was a final dull *thud* as it exploded in the bushes, with pieces flying in all directions.

Now as chance would have it, a hare happened to be resting under those bushes and when the big egg came crashing down, the frightened hare sprang out and took to his heels.

The settler saw the hare and immediately thought it was his long-awaited colt that had finally been released from the egg.

He started scrambling through the brambles, frantically looking for the young horse and calling:

"Wee-haw coltie . . . I'm your fadder! . . . Come to me coltie, come to me!! Wee-haw. Come to me."

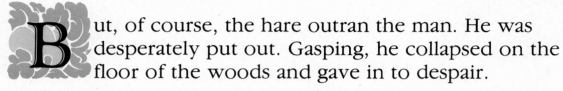

But, of course, the hare outran the man. He was desperately put out. Gasping, he collapsed on the floor of the woods and gave in to despair.

He had lost his money.

He had spent all autumn sitting on a big orange egg and now he had lost his colt.

He would never have a horse.

ut then, as his breath came back to him, he began to recall the many things his neighbours had told him about horses.

"My, my," he thought. "He had terrible big ears. Terrible big ears for a colt that size. He would have been balky, that's for sure!"

"And his teeth," he thought, "I caught a glimpse of his teeth. He would have bitten me . . . maybe hurt me badly."

And finally he said, "Come to think of it, he was terrible low in the hindquarters. He would have kicked like a son-of-a-gun!"

etting up and dusting himself off, the settler
decided he was a very lucky man indeed. "For sure,
for sure, he was a runaway. I would have fed him and
trained him and then he would have left as soon as I turned my
back. It was better that he got away from me at the very start. I'm
far, far better off without such a beast."

So the little man walked back to his cabin, whistling a happy tune to himself and feeling very much better about the whole adventure. The more he thought about it, the better he felt.

In no time at all he could save up ten dollars for another egg, and ten dollars was surely not too much to pay for the perfect horse.

CAROLE SPRAY, of Fredericton, New Brunswick, is the author of *Will O' The Wisp,* a collection of Canadian folk tales and legends. A mother of two, and a former elementary school teacher, children's librarian and creative writing instructor, Carole has received an Explorations grant from the Canada Council and has spent the last five years collecting, transcribing and editing tapes of Eastern Canada's folklore.

KIM LA FAVE is one of Canada's outstanding young illustrators, with several national awards to his credit. A native of Vancouver transplanted to Toronto, and a graduate of The Alberta College of Art, Kim was at the kitchen table drawing on writing pads and brown paper bags as far back as his first memories. Clearly recalling favourite childhood books, especially the Beatrix Potter series, he has long been drawn to the field of children's book illustration. When not painting in the cramped, spare bedroom of the apartment where he lives with his wife, Carol Snelling, also a painter, Kim likes to get out in the open to ski, swim or "rat around on a dirt bike."

## Impelled By Despair

They came by the hundreds, by the thousands and finally by the millions: between 1800 and 1875, more than 7,500,000 people left for the New World from the British Isles alone. By 1828, 30,000 a year were crossing. They came in large ships and in small ships, in sound ships and in ships so rotten that they sometimes sank before they were out of sight of Britain. They came in the comfortable and expensive cabins, and they came jammed like sardines into the holds of returning timber ships that were not designed to carry human beings at all.

People emigrated because they had to. In Scotland, those who owned the land, the lairds or those who had bought the lairds out, found that sheep were more profitable than people, and the Highland clansmen were driven away. The weather, too, played a part. The summer of 1816 was cold and wet, crops failed, and famine forced many out. The English middle classes and tradesmen were also hard hit by the end of the Napoleonic Wars. Many petty officers and soldiers were out of work and had no other career to fall back on. In Ireland, although the potato famine had not yet struck, hunger was habitual. The British government encouraged emigration.

In Britain, only the rich owned land. In the colonies, it was said, even a poor man might, by hard labour and perseverance, obtain a little land that he could actually *own*, not rent or work for someone else. This was the one thing that would make the voyage worth it.

## Conditions In Steerage

That is, if you could survive the voyage. Many didn't. For poor men or women, the voyage across the Atlantic in the steerage of a sailing ship was likely to be as close to hell as they would ever come. Once you had set sail, there was no turning back. You would already have sold what little property you might possess in order to pay for your fare and for your food for the voyage. Your fare would have been cheap enough, but what it bought you was miserable.

From the moment he embarked, a steerage passenger in a bad ship would be surrounded by the stench of bilge, vomit, smoke from what little cooking would be done, decaying food, and human excrement. In such close quarters, disease was common. Cholera, dysentery and typhus, once on board, often ran through the entire ship. A few emigrants literally died of starvation. Others developed scurvy. Water, too, was a problem. Ships were supposed to carry a minimum of fifty-two gallons of water per person, but few owners obeyed this regulation. Sometimes the water was tainted before the ship even set out, and when the casks were opened they were found to be covered with greenish scum. You had to be made of stern stuff to survive a crossing in the steerage of a "coffin" ship: dank, dark, stinking compartments, overrun with lice and rats, where food was old and uncooked, and cutpurses enjoyed easy picking.

## Depends On Who You Are

Although a lady in the cabin could get just as seasick as a crofter's wife in the steerage, life in the cabin was definitely more enjoyable. Dinner was at four, and while the cabin passengers ate, the steerage passengers may have been allowed up on deck. William Powell, who crossed in 1834 and kept an effervescent journal, describes a meal:

*We generally sat down about thirty in number, the cap'n presiding of course, and during the first part of the voyage we had fresh beef and all the time we were at sea which was about five weeks our mess was furnished with fresh mutton, pork, (both very good) geese, fowls, &c. (bad) salt-beef (not junk) tongues, hams, potatoes, soups, (all very good). These formed the first course. The second course consisted of puddings of various sorts, plum, rice and custard, preserved cranberry, gooseberry and cherry tarts. With these and a few glasses of sherry or champagne we managed to get along tolerably well. For dessert we had oranges, almonds and raisins, nuts and hickory nuts, figs and many other little dainties over which and the wine of four or five different kinds, we generally passed away a couple of hours amusing ourselves indifferently well.*

But rich or poor, cabin or steerage, there were some dangers emigrants had in common. If the steerage had cholera, the cabin was threatened. If the ship sank, all would drown. And all alike were subject to theft. Books for emigrants repeatedly warned against this. Even potatoes should be kept in barrels with locks. If the ship did make the voyage without disease, it might find a plague raging in the port, brought by some previous ship.

At Quebec, during the cholera plague of 1832, passengers were required to land at Grosse Isle for "purification." (Cabin passengers did not have to get purified in person: they could send a servant with the bedding.) The emigrants were supposed to wash themselves, their clothing and their bedding in the river. Men and boys, jubilant after long confinement, leapt into the river; women tucked up their skirts and tramped their bedding "in tubs or in holes in the rocks." Susanna Moodie, an emigrant and writer, could not understand why the people were behaving in such an uproarious way, running around half-naked and "cutting antics that would surprise the leader of a circus." Perhaps if she had just spent seven weeks in the steerage she would have understood.

## Hopes and Fears

If Britain had not been the Garden of Eden, neither were the colonies. Still, they were not a total desert either, and for a poor man, they offered one thing which Europe could

no longer offer: hope. Those who had survived the crossing, the disease, the hunger and the human jackals, had something to look forward to.

"Whurrah! my boys," Mrs. Moodie heard an Irishman shouting, "Shure we'll all be jintlemen!" The promised land, or the land where land was promised, had been reached. These Scottish crofters, English farm labourers and Irish potato growers, without a hope of owning land at home, could become masters of their own destiny in the colonies, provided they worked hard enough. First they had to spend months cutting brush, felling trees, tugging at stumps and lugging rocks off the heavily forested land. Only then could they plant — and the lives of their families would depend on the success of that first crop.

On the other hand, the fear uppermost in the minds of another whole class of British emigrants — the impoverished gentlefolk, those younger sons of good families, half-pay officers and minor officials whose sinecures had become obsolete — was that by going to the Canadas and dipping their hands into the soil, they would lose class. Their foremost hope was that they would be able to recoup their fallen fortunes and gain a social position equal to the one they felt by rights to be theirs. Visions of landed gentry danced in their heads. But of this class of emigrant, few were the sensible Catherine Parr Traills. Most were like Catherine's accomplished and helpless sister, Susanna Moodie.

## Natural Targets

In the late twenties and thirties, such people poured into British North America by the thousands. These people were naive, ignorant of the perils awaiting them, unused to physical labour, class conscious and proud. Thus they were natural targets for cheats and profiteers, and many of them failed miserably. Their worst fears were realized; the sons of poor gentlemen generally lost caste and sunk into useless sots, while those of the lower classes, more used to privation and toil, were able to rise above them.

###  Astonishing The Neighbours

From a distance it all seemed so easy. Once in the colonies, all you had to do was locate your land grant, if you had one, or purchase a farm if you didn't. If the land was partially cleared, with buildings already on it, your task was simple. You would put in a crop, clear more land and convert the trees to potash or timber, start increasing your livestock, and make English improvements, such as corn stands, five-barred gates, hay stacks and sheep pens, which would astonish the neighbours.

Needless to say, your work would be mainly supervisory; there would be hired hands to do the actual physical labour. In the winters everyone would have fun sleighing and skating and the evenings would pass with the family and equally genteel neighbours gathered 'round the blazing hearth, singing, playing the flute, reading aloud, drawing, or playing chess or backgammon. The land would be fertile and the weather something like England's, though with hotter summers and snowier winters.

###  Ignorance And Gullibility

In reality, the middle-class English emigrants were more likely to astonish their neighbours by their ignorance and gullibility than by their improvements. Many were the ex-army officers who transported their families across the Atlantic only to find that their grants were not in the fertile, flat and balmy regions but in a swamp, on a rocky hillside or on a ridge of sand. The friendly land agents they were anticipating may have proved to be more like the artful seducers and rogues the Moodies encountered. The climate was unexpectedly harsh and the exhausting toil unending. In addition to the cooking, baking, preserving, soap making, kitchen-gardening, butchering and meat curing, candle making, spinning, sugar making, dairy and poultry work, rule-of-thumb doctoring and midwifery, there was the backbreaking clearing and making potash, building, fencing and putting in crops. English gentlefolk were simply incapable of such feats, and their farms often failed because they lacked the supply of unpaid labour necessary to turn a profit.

###  Bedevilled By Neighbours

And if you did fail, many of the neighbours would cheer. The educated classes were unprepared for the malice and vindictiveness of the Yankee squatters or working-class British emigrants around them, who regarded the genteel English as fools and dupes and greatly resented their old-country customs and assumptions of superiority.

For example, although Mrs. Moodie was not from a rich family, she, like everyone of her class, had taken servants for granted. In the New World, their servants were always deserting at crucial moments, leaving Mrs. Moodie to face some frightening task on her own. She was terrified the first time she had to milk a cow. She had never done a washing before she came to Canada, and the first time she attempted to heat water for one she almost smoked herself and her family out of the house. She didn't know how to dry apples, so lost her whole crop to an old woman who offered to do it for her and then stole the results.

The Moodies were bedevilled by their neighbours, who tricked them, sneered at them, and borrowed everything the Moodies were stupid enough to lend. When they moved from their first shack into a bigger log house, they found that the vacating tenants had girdled all the orchard trees, flooded their floor and hidden a dead skunk in their mantelpiece.

The amazing thing is not that so many of these genteel settlers folded up, but that so many made it through.

Margaret Atwood
*condensed from Days of the Rebels*